Space Explorer

LIVING IN SPACE

Patricia Whitehouse

Heinemann Library
Chicago, Illinois

Designed by Heinemann Library

Printed in China by South China Printing.

08 07 06 05 04

10 9 8 7 6 5 4 3 2 1

Library of Congress Cataloging-in-Publication Data

Whitehouse, Patricia, 1958-

   Living in space / Patricia Whitehouse.

       v. cm. -- (Space explorer)

   Includes bibliographical references and index.

   Contents: Leaving earth -- Living in microgravity -- Breathing
in space -- Getting water -- What to wear -- Eating in space --
Keeping clean -- Taking out the trash -- Having fun -- Keeping
fit -- Sleeping in space -- Living in space in the future --
Amazing space facts.

   ISBN 1-4034-5151-6 (Library Binding-hardcover) -- ISBN 1-
4034-5655-0 (Paperback)

   1. Life support systems (Space environment)--Juvenile
literature. [1. Space shuttles. 2. Space stations. 3. Manned
space flights. 4. Astronauts.] I. Title. II. Series.

   TL1500.W49 2004

   629.47'7--dc22

2003026762

Acknowledgments

The author and publishers are grateful to the following for
permission to reproduce copyright material:

Cover photograph: NASA

p. 4 Photodisk; p. 5 NASA; p. 6 NASA; p. 7 NASA;
p. 8 NASA; p. 9 NASA; p. 10 NASA; p. 11 NASA;
p. 12 NASA; p. 13 Topham/Photri; p. 14 NASA;
p. 15 NASA; p. 16 NASA; p. 17 NASA; p. 18 NASA;
p. 19 Science Photo Library; p. 20 NASA; p. 21 NASA;
p. 22 NASA; p. 23 Roger Ressmayer/NASA/Corbis;
p. 24 NASA; p. 25 Science Photo Library; p. 26 NASA;
p. 27 NASA; p. 28 NASA; p. 29 NASA

Every effort has been made to contact copyright holders of any
material reproduced in this book. Any omissions will be
rectified in subsequent printings if notice is given to the
publisher.

Special thanks to Geza Gyuk of the Adler Planetarium for his
comments in preparation of this book.

Some words are shown in bold, **like this.** You can find out
what they mean by looking in the glossary.

Contents

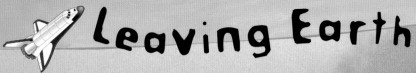# Leaving Earth

Five, four, three, two, one—the space shuttle blasts off! The seven **astronauts** on the shuttle are away from Earth and into space.

4

Three of the seven astronauts will live at the International **Space Station** for 90 days. Astronauts go into space to learn how it is different from Earth.

Before they leave Earth, the astronauts learn how to work, eat, and sleep in space.

The shuttle has two **decks.** The lower deck is used for eating and sleeping. The upper deck is used for **experiments.** This is also where most of the shuttle's controls are.

This astronaut is checking an experiment.

On the International Space Station,
experiments and controls cover the walls.

The International **Space Station** is
much larger than a space shuttle. It has
bedrooms, a kitchen, a science lab, and
a radio center. When it is finished, it
will be as big as three houses.

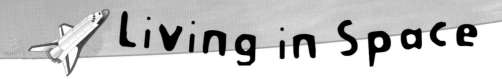

Living in Space

The space shuttle travels around Earth so fast that it is like falling. Everything inside falls, too. It makes **astronauts** and everything in the shuttle float around. This is called weightlessness.

A special airplane ride gives astronauts the feeling of weightlessness.

Eating, sleeping, and moving are different in space. Astronauts practice these activities before leaving Earth.

9

Breathing in Space

Because there is no air in space, **astronauts** need to bring and make their own. When astronauts leave the space shuttle, they wear air tanks so they can breathe.

air tanks

Astronauts need to breathe clean
air on the space station.

On the **space station,** machines use
water to make air. Other machines
keep the air clean. Sometimes the air
gets pretty smelly!

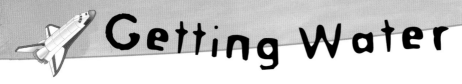

There is no water in space, either. The space shuttle carries water in tanks. **Astronauts** are careful about how much water they use because they do not want it to run out.

Water is stored in tanks like this.

In space, special machines like this one clean all the dirty water.

Astronauts do not throw away any water. Instead, they **recycle** it. Machines clean the water so it can be used again. Space water is probably cleaner than the water from your faucet.

hook-and-loop-fastener

Astronauts wear shirts and pants or shorts. The pants and shorts have hook-and-loop fastener strips for attaching tools. Astronauts from the **space station** send their dirty clothes back to Earth on the space shuttle.

Astronauts wear special suits during launch and landing. These suits protect them in case of emergencies. When they work outside, astronauts wear spacesuits that cover their whole bodies.

These astronauts are in their special suits, ready to return to Earth.

Eating in Space

In space **astronauts** eat many of the same foods that they eat on Earth. But they do not eat bread because it makes too many crumbs.

Food is packed so it will not float away.

Astronauts drink coffee, tea, milk, or juice. Drinks start out as powder in a bag. Astronauts add water to the bag to make their drink.

Astronauts drink through a special straw.

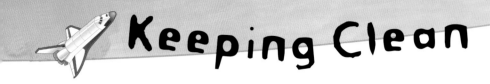

Keeping Clean

Astronauts cannot shower in space. The water would float away! Instead, they use a soapy towel to wash. They brush their teeth the same way as they do on Earth.

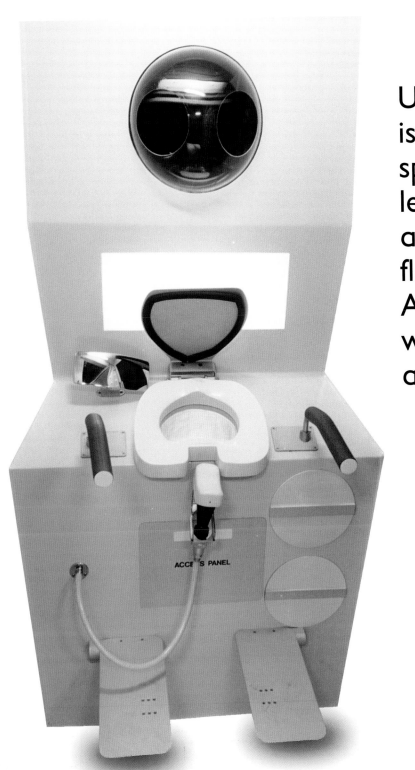

ACCESS PANEL

Using the toilet is different in space. Foot and leg holders keep astronauts from floating away. Air jets push waste into a tank.

Taking Out the Garbag

Leftover food and waste paper become garbage. A very small amount of garbage gets thrown out of the **space station.** It is thrown out carefully so that it does not come back and hit the space station.

This garbage will be thrown into space.

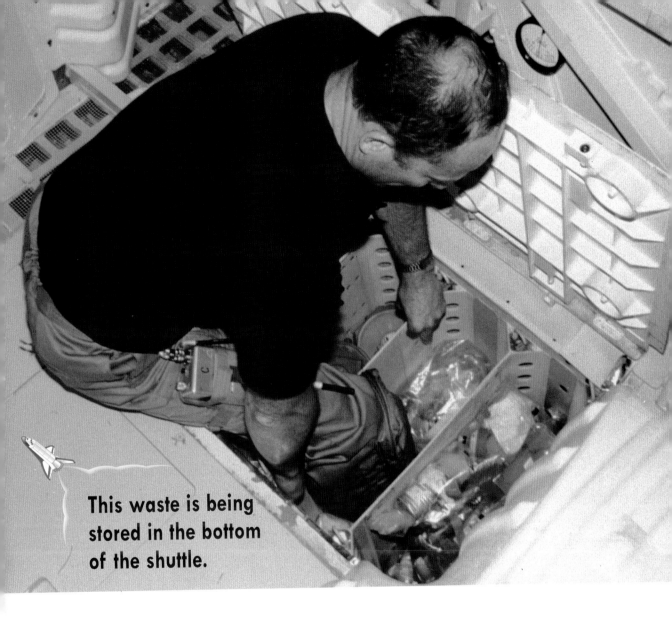

This waste is being stored in the bottom of the shuttle.

Other trash is put on the lowest deck of the shuttle. It lands with the shuttle and is **recycled** or thrown away on Earth.

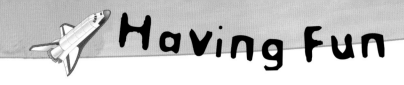

Having Fun

Astronauts have jobs to do in space, but there is time to relax. They can read books, watch movies, or listen to music.

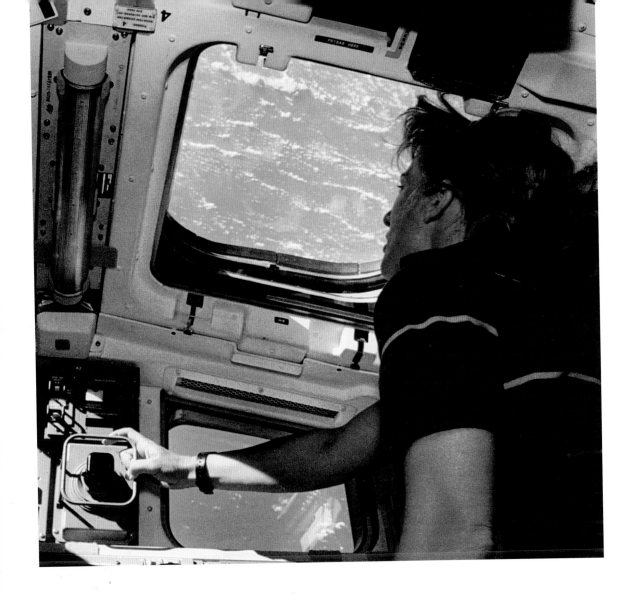

Being in space is fun. Astronauts enjoy floating around. It is also exciting to look out of the window at Earth.

Keeping Fit

In space, **astronauts** do not use their muscles or bones very much. Their bones and muscles can get too weak to work properly when they return to Earth. So they exercise every day.

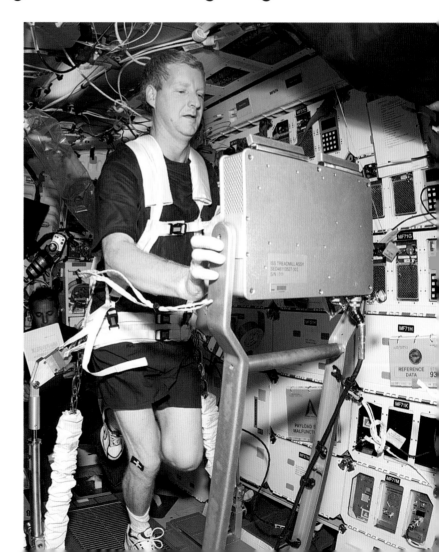

Running makes astronauts use their bones and muscles and helps them stay strong.

Astronauts use **treadmills,** exercise bikes, and rowing machines to stay in shape. They need to strap themselves onto the machines so they do not float away.

Sleeping in Space

Astronauts sleep in sleeping bags. The bags have to be tied to bunk beds, seats, or the wall. Otherwise, the sleeping astronauts would float around the **space station!**

It is hard to fall asleep in space. The Sun shines on the space station every 90 minutes. Fans and machines make noises. Some astronauts need to sleep with masks and earplugs.

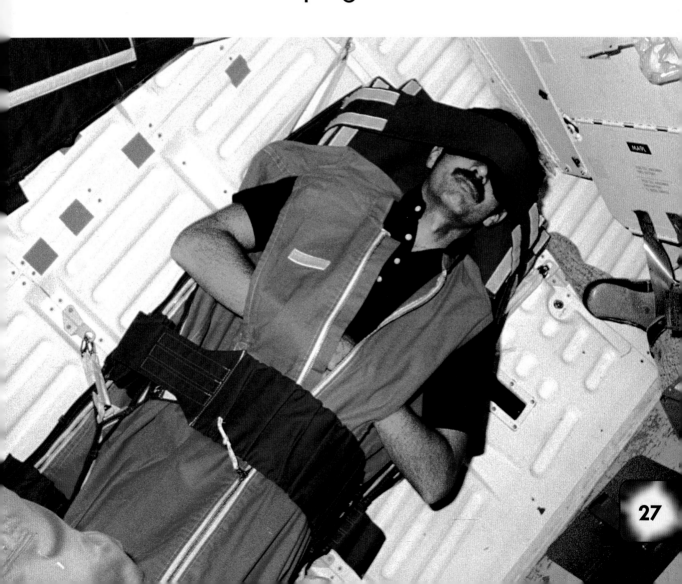

The Future

In the future, people might travel long distances in space. But scientists must find a way to supply food, air, and water for a long trip.

This is a drawing of what space stations might look like in the future.

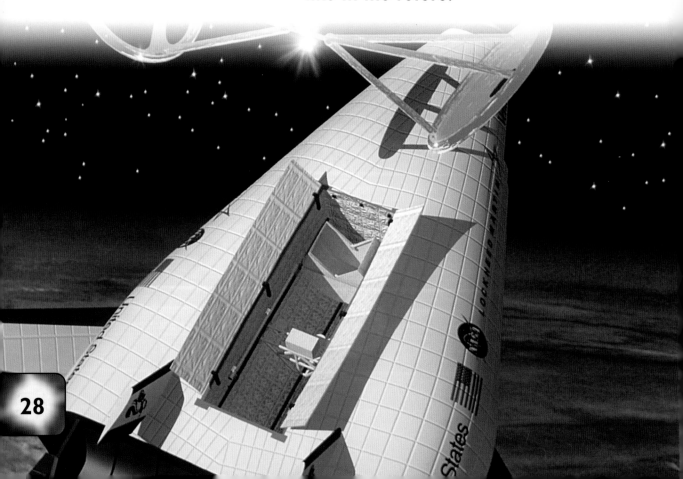

To live on another planet, people would need a lot of equipment. This drawing shows what it might look like.

Today, people cannot live on any planet besides the Earth. But scientists believe that people might be able to live on other planets in the future.

 Amazing Space Facts

In 2003, Yuri Malenchenko became the first person to get married while in space. His bride, Kat Dmitriev, was on Earth for the wedding, so they used a video to see each other.

The first meal in space was eaten by the **astronaut** Scott Carpenter in 1962. He ate apple sauce squeezed from a tube.

Astronauts get to choose which food they want to eat. Their food packages are marked so they do not get mixed up with anyone else's.

Glossary

astronaut person who goes into space

deck level

experiment test

recycle to change waste or unwanted things into material that can be used again

space station a place where astronauts work and live in space

treadmill exercise equipment that allows a person to walk or run in one place

More Books to Read

Whitehouse, Patricia. *Space Equipment (Space Explorer)*. Chicago: Heinemann Library, 2004.

Whitehouse, Patricia. *Space Travel (Space Explorer)*. Chicago: Heinemann Library, 2004.

Whitehouse, Patricia. *Working in Space (Space Explorer)*. Chicago: Heinemann Library, 2004.

Index